AUTOBIOGRA

- PRISON DC

MYRON FOUNTAINE

ISBN 979-8-89145-471-2

Leedspublishing.com

Twitter.com/leedspresscorp

Instagram.com/leedspresscorp

Facebook.com/leedspresscorp

Printed in the United States of America

CONTENTS

DEDICATION

Dedicated to my son Eli M. Fountaine

May you always seek knowledge and your

purpose in life.

PREFACE

With over a 90% success rate at transforming troubled children, I pray that this book will aid all families at building better relationships with their children.

Some of my most unforgettable house calls:

I will never forget the 78-year-old grandmother who was so afraid of her out of control 9-year-old grandson that she didn't want him to find out that she contacted me for help. She was being physically abused and put in chokeholds by her grandson.

I will never forget the 8-year-old who slapped his grandmother so hard her glasses flew across the room, and he left a bruise under her eye.

I will never forget the 5-year-old who calls his mother B's and H's like it was her name!

I have made thousands of house calls for troubled children throughout my 10-year career and over 70% were of single parent homes.

Many of these parents have exhausted all their resources and feel completely helpless. Children have learned how to weaponize the police against their own parents in order to get their way.

Parental Tips

1. Never let your children see that you're afraid of them. When they detect fear in you, they will constantly bully you to get their way.

2. Be the law in your home and be ready to hand down consequences for breaking the law in your home. All children at their core desires discipline and structure even in their madness

3. Change your energy. If your child(ren) constantly sees you down and out, depressed and defeated it can create insecurities and feelings of abandonment in your child(ren).

4. Lead by example. The old thinking of "do as I say and not as I do" doesn't work on our children today, it never did. Children will imitate what they see.

5. Spend quality time with your child(ren) every day to build trust and understanding

6. Both parents need to be present in their child's lives. Children need love from their mothers and fathers.

7. Teach them while they're young about aim and purpose and spirituality.

PRISON DOCTOR   MYRON FOUNTANE

.

INTRODUCTION

My name is Myron Fountaine, and I grew up on the west side of Detroit, in the Dexter Davison area, a place affectionately known as Motown. I was born on May 9, 1967. In the sixties, the city of Detroit was bustling with a musical revolution; at the pick of it was the famous record label Motown Records. It was a time characterized by creativity, passion, and cultural transformation among African Americans across the United States, and music was at the heart of this revolution.

Detroit earned the nickname "Motor City" due to its pivotal role in the rise of the American automobile industry. Companies like Ford Motors, Buick, Cadillac, Chevrolet, and GMC, later merging into General Motors (G.M.) and Chrysler, quickly became the bedrock of American industrialization. This reputation was solidified by a convergence of key factors that made Detroit the epicenter of automotive innovation and manufacturing during the early to mid-20th century.

At the heart of Detroit's transformation into the Motor City was the visionary genius of individuals like Henry Ford. His introduction of the assembly line production technique revolutionized manufacturing processes, enabling vehicles to be produced at an unprecedented speed and efficiency. Ford's Model T, introduced in 1908, became a symbol of the accessible automobile, making cars affordable and attainable for a broader range of consumers.

The city's strategic geographical location also played a vital role. At the nexus of waterways and railroads, Detroit had excellent access to raw materials such as steel, rubber, and glass, essential for automobile production. This geographical advantage reduced transportation costs and facilitated the swift movement of materials to assembly plants.

Moreover, Detroit's established manufacturing infrastructure, initially built around the production of carriages and bicycles, seamlessly transitioned to automobile manufacturing. Skilled labor from these existing industries contributed to developing a workforce with the expertise needed for building automobiles.

The early establishment of major automobile companies further propelled Detroit's reputation. Industry giants like Ford, General Motors, and Chrysler set up headquarters and manufacturing facilities in the city, attracting talent and investment. This concentration of automotive expertise fostered a competitive environment that spurred continuous innovation, driving technological advancements in the field.

As the city's automotive industry grew, it became a major driver of the local economy. The creation of countless jobs drew individuals from various regions, leading to a population boom and urban expansion. This economic prosperity, in turn, attracted more industry players and suppliers, establishing a self-reinforcing growth cycle.

The combination of these factors culminated in Detroit's identification as the Motor City. It symbolized not only the epicenter of automobile manufacturing but also the embodiment of American ingenuity, industrial prowess, and economic vitality. The moniker encapsulated Detroit's status as the birthplace of mass production techniques, the home of iconic automobile brands, and the engine behind the transformation of personal transportation.

Let's talk about Black People, my people. The Great Migration of black people to Detroit occurred primarily between the early 20th century and the mid-20th century, driven by a combination of push and pull factors that reshaped the city's demographic landscape.

The "push" factors were the difficult circumstances faced by black communities in the Southern United States. People of color had been working on farms picking cotton, raising animals, and doing various manual labor jobs without pay. The South was, therefore, deeply entrenched in racial segregation, systemic racism, economic disparities, and a lack of opportunities for upward mobility. Widespread racial violence, such as lynching and discriminatory laws, created a hostile environment for black individuals and families. Seeking to escape these conditions, many black people began to look for better prospects in other parts of the country.

The "pull" factors were the promises of better opportunities and living conditions in the North, including cities like Detroit. The burgeoning industrialization and economic growth in cities presented the allure of jobs in factories and industries. Northern cities were often seen as places with less overt racial discrimination and a chance for a better quality of life. Black people understood clearly that there was always an undertone of racism in the North since not all white people embraced Blacks. The good news was that Blacks could get wages for their labor at the minimum, which was way better than the free labor they had experienced in the South.

The onset of World War I and World War II significantly accelerated this migration. Many American Youths, especially whites, had been drafted into the military during these wars. Needless to point out, many of them were killed in battle. So, there was an obvious shortage of labor. The wars, this led to a high demand for labor in industries. Hence the need for workers in most industries, regardless of race, color, or gender. Black individuals saw these opportunities as a chance to escape the harsh conditions of the South and pursue better prospects in cities like Detroit.

The journey to Detroit was often arduous, with many black migrants traveling long distances by train or bus. When they arrived, they faced both challenges and opportunities. While Detroit offered better jobs and relative freedom from the harsh segregation laws of the South, it was not without racial tensions. The influx of black workers sometimes led to competition for jobs and housing, which occasionally resulted in clashes with white residents.

The black migrants to Detroit settled primarily in neighborhoods like Black Bottom and Paradise Valley, where they established vibrant communities and contributed to the cultural and economic fabric of the city. They worked in industries such as automotive manufacturing, booming during this period. They played a significant role in fueling Detroit's growth as the Motor City.

Despite these challenges, black people and their descendants persevered, contributing to Detroit's social, cultural, and economic development while also fighting for civil rights and equality in the face of ongoing racial discrimination and segregation. So, one of those contributions was music. Music runs deep in the Black community. They have sung songs while working, even as slaves. They passed messages from one to another, including how to escape from the South, using songs and rhythms.

In Detroit, that tradition continued as well. Black people found a way to create their own entertainment. In the church, they had choirs. The preacher could sing while he preached; mothers would sing beautiful lullabies to their children. After a hard day at work on the assembly lines in

Detroit, Black people would gather at the clubs they founded and enjoy themselves, dancing their nights away.

It was during this period that a young saxophonist named Eli Fountaine emerged. This young man is my father. To this day, he's the source of my inspiration. Gifted with a natural musical talent, Eli honed his skills and embraced the soulful sounds that permeated the city. As Motown Records rose to prominence, Eli was drawn to the label's unique style and innovative approach to music-making. His saxophone was the introduction to many songs. He would ignite the crowd and set the mood and tempo for the night. Whenever his lips touched the horn, the place went quiet in anticipation of his genius notes.

Motown Records, under the visionary leadership of Berry Gordy Jr., became a mecca for talented artists seeking to make their mark on the world stage. The label's headquarters, affectionately known as Hitsville U.S.A., served as the creative hub where countless iconic songs were recorded. Within these hallowed walls, my father's saxophone would lend its distinctive voice to the Motown sound.

My father's mastery of the saxophone brought an extra layer of depth and emotion to the music created at Motown; soulful melodies intertwined with infectious rhythms and captivating harmonies elevate the songs to new heights. His saxophone became integral to the Motown legacy, whether the smooth jazz-infused tunes or the energetic bursts of soul.

Collaborating with Motown's legendary artists and musicians, my father's saxophone resonated with passion, skill, and sheer musicality. He contributed his talents to numerous recordings, adding a touch of brilliance to the iconic songs that defined an era. From Marvin Gaye's heartfelt ballads to Stevie Wonder's infectious grooves, his saxophone became a recognizable element of the Motown sound.

Beyond the studio, my father's performances captivated audiences in live shows and tours. His soul-stirring solos left an indelible impression on listeners, eliciting emotions and evoking a sense of joy and nostalgia. Whether taking center stage or supporting his fellow Motown artists, my father's saxophone became a conduit for the heart and soul of the music.

The Motown era in Detroit was a time of cultural significance and artistic innovation. With his exceptional talent and unwavering dedication, my father played an instrumental role in shaping the Motown sound. His contributions, on record and live performances, resonate with music lovers worldwide.

As the legacy of Motown endures, My father's saxophone remains a symbol of the creativity and passion that defined an era. His artistry lives on, reminding us of the timeless beauty and power of music born in the heart of Detroit.

My father had an impeccable reputation as a professional and was the best father I could have ever asked for. His saxophone was behind the opening musical solo on "What's Going On " and the very first notes on the albums "Mercy, Mercy Me " and "Inner City Blues." The horn you hear on those songs is my dad's. He also played with The Dramatics and discovered them in the early sixties and many other famous Motown groups. My father is my ultimate inspiration. He is the first person I ever saw as a celebrity or a famous individual because he had a larger-than-life personality, genuinely respected and loved by many people.

But my strength comes from my mother, Janet, my hero. She taught me the meaning of love, discipline, and hard work. Despite my father being on tour most of the time, my mother ensured we were well-fed and cared for. She raised us almost like a single mother would. When Dad wasn't touring with Motown, he had to practice for the next tour or fulfill other duties at the music studio. Being a musician, I later learned, is a very demanding profession. He was gone more days, than he was home with us. My father would often be in the studios working or playing gigs at places like The Latin Quarters, a famous club in Detroit. A little bit of history here, Latin Quarter was a historic nightclub in Detroit that played a significant role in the city's entertainment and cultural scene. Opening its doors in the 1940s, the Latin Quarter quickly became a vibrant and influential hub for music, dancing, and socializing. The club was notable for its diverse lineup of performers, energetic atmosphere, and contribution to the city's rich musical heritage.

Situated in the heart of Detroit's entertainment district, The Latin Quarter attracted a diverse crowd, including locals and visitors. The club's name reflected its ambiance, often featuring Latin music and dance styles, adding a unique flavor to the city's nightlife. However, The Latin Quarter was not limited to just Latin music; it hosted various musical acts, including jazz, rhythm and blues, and rock 'n' roll artists, contributing to Detroit's reputation as a musical hotspot.

The Latin Quarter became particularly prominent during the 1950s and 1960s, a period of significant social change and musical innovation. Many renowned musicians and bands graced the club's stage, contributing to its legendary status. Performers such as Sammy Davis Jr., Sarah Vaughan, and Jackie Wilson were among the artists who entertained audiences at the Latin Quarter, solidifying its reputation as a premier entertainment venue.

Beyond its musical offerings, the Latin Quarter also fostered a sense of community and brought people together. The club's lively dance floor and social atmosphere provided a space for people to connect, celebrate, and enjoy a night out. It contributed to the cultural fabric of Detroit and added to the city's vibrant social scene.

As time passed, the Latin Quarter, like many historic venues such as the 20 grand which is where my mother and father met and another staple in the Detroit music scene, faced changes and challenges. The club eventually closed its doors, marking the end of an era. However, its legacy lives on through the memories of those who experienced its vibrant performances and unique ambiance. The Latin Quarter remains part of Detroit's cultural history, representing a time when music, dance, and social interaction converged to create unforgettable moments in the city's nightlife. It was not surprising that my mother understood the significance of the club and why my father performed and frequented it.

My mother wasn't just a devoted mother; she also pursued education in the medical field and became a licensed practical nurse (L.P.N.), working at Mount Carmel and Mercy Hospitals. Back then, nurses were revered as they formed the frontlines in many medical institutions. In the Black community, nurses were needed for everything from midwives to first responders in many medical emergencies. Her hard work ethic and leadership qualities earned her a great reputation as a nurse. She primarily raised my four brothers and me together, and she did a marvelous job.

As I grew older, I accompanied my father on many trips everywhere. I witnessed firsthand the admiration and popularity he received. Although my mother disapproved of the music industry's impact on their marriage, she remained a dedicated nurse and a loving mother to me and my siblings. She also understood what came with musicians. The constant travels around the country touring and the demand to constantly perform put its toll on their marriage. And since my parents had children, my mother opted to work and raise us from home. She did not tour with my father. Especially being a nurse and having the community needing her services as well.

Growing up, my childhood in Detroit was enjoyable, safe, and structured. Like many kids my age, I would head out to play after finishing school and homework, returning home when the streetlights turned on. I was a good kid, stayed mostly out of trouble, and excelled in sports, particularly football, softball, and dodgeball. I even earned the M.V.P. title in my neighborhood. However, being popular had its own challenges. Peer pressure made me associate with the wrong crowd, and I started my wrongdoing.

I remember when it started. I stole some money from my mother's purse to buy candy. On the surface, many kids did this, and it was acceptable. Still, it created a thrill of getting away with it, so I became addicted. As they say, a bad habit is hard to get rid of. I then escalated to stealing a scooter and, ultimately, a car. One day, my friends and I impulsively decided to steal a white Mustang convertible. Armed with a knife, we approached the owner and demanded the car keys. Though we managed to escape with the stolen car, our joy ride ended abruptly when I crashed the vehicle while trying to evade the police. This resulted in my arrest, conviction for vehicular armed robbery, and a 25–50-year sentence in Michigan's state prison.

When I got arrested and sentenced, everyone who knew me and my family was shocked and devastated. It was difficult for many people to understand how coming from a loving and successful family, I could end up in prison for a crime that never needed to be done in the first place. We were not poor and most definitely not lacking money or the means to live a decent life. However, I held onto my faith, studying religious texts and seeking wisdom from a higher power to cope with the harsh and lonely prison life.

Visits from my mother provided comfort during my time in prison but witnessing her endure humiliating searches before entering the visiting room made me feel ashamed. Despite her disapproval of my situation, she remained a devoted mother, ensuring I had the money I needed, encouraging me to stay connected with her, and focusing on my spiritual growth.

I felt the shame that I brought my family. I knew that I could've done things differently. Seeing my mother's sadness made me feel worse because I knew she had to hide it to face me in prison. Like many parents, they ask themselves, "Where did I go wrong with my son?" These thoughts bothered me a lot in that lonely cell at night. I could feel my father's anguish and how he must have felt. He took me everywhere. I met so many celebrities of his time. And yet here I was with no family but strangers and criminals who, only God knew what they had done before getting caught. I held on to the hope that one day my redemption would come. But time has its own ways of making you wait.

Prison life felt monotonous, with the same routines and lack of freedom every day. I used all available resources, participating in self-help groups, visiting the library, and exercising at the weight pit to break the monotony and find some purpose. I had to survive; I needed to live life no matter how much pressure the confinement in a small cell and a backyard provided. We were crowded sometimes, everyone had to be out for the usual breaks, and all activities went on.

I reflected on my actions and felt deep remorse, guilt, and shame for my carjacking crime. While acknowledging my deserving place in prison, I couldn't help but question the disproportionally lenient sentences for other crimes, such as sexual offenses. Nevertheless, I maintained hope for a better future, believing in my capacity for greatness and my determination to prove it.

CHAPTER 1
SOUND CHECK BACKSTAGE ACCESS AND MY CHILDHOOD

My dad was frequently away from home during my childhood, especially when my brothers and I were growing up. Nevertheless, when he returned, he always took me on his adventures. As the youngest in our family, I distinctly remember the moments between the ages of ten and thirteen when my father whisked me away with him wherever he went. Being the son of a well-known Motown musician came with certain advantages. I accompanied him to numerous studios and bars in Detroit, Michigan. These experiences allowed me to meet and interact with many renowned entertainers, which impacted my young mind.

I have a clear memory of meeting the singing group members, The Dramatics, and legendary figures like Smokey Robinson, Barry Gordy, and Diana Ross. The memory of Diana Ross kissing my cheek when I was a young child is something

I will never forget. I also consider myself fortunate to have had the opportunity to meet talented artists such as Phyllis Hyman and Denise Williams. Denise Williams, in particular, was always kind and showered me with affection and compliments.

One of my most special moments was when Mr. James Brown, famously known as "the hardest working man in show business," gave me a bike in either 1976 or 1977. I still recall the excitement of accompanying my dad to a sound check at the Masonic Temple in Detroit. Watching the band members rehearse on stage left me in awe, and then, to my surprise, James Brown called me up and presented me with a birthday gift on the side of the stage. It was a Schwinn bike, colored yellow and black, adorned with special features.

However, my enthusiasm led to a mishap when I rode the bike too fast and dented the front wheel. Without fully understanding the value of the gift, I attempted to fix it by changing the tire, but my efforts were futile. My frustration got better, and I discarded the bike in the backyard. When my mother found out, she rightfully expressed her displeasure and explained the significance and sentiment behind the gift. That day taught me a valuable lesson, and I faced a memorable punishment. Nevertheless, it remains a cherished memory of the influential people who positively impacted my life.

Growing up as the son of a prominent Motown musician, I had the privilege of meeting and knowing every Motown artist imaginable. My father's connections granted me the freedom to explore Motown Records and United Sound System Studios, two of Michigan's largest studios. Motown hosted well-known artists like Marvin Gaye, Smokey Robinson, The Supremes, and The Temptations. United Sound System Studios featured names like Michael Henderson, The Dramatics, Isaac Hayes, and Stevie Wonder. My father was not only a skilled horn player for Motown but also held the position of vice president at United Sound System Studios, earning him respect and admiration within the music industry.

My dad was my ultimate hero, with his musical talent and affectionate nature. His presence in my life opened doors to exceptional experiences. I hold dear every moment spent with him, where I learned from his expertise and witnessed his significant impact on the music world.

CHAPTER 2
GOING TO PRISON

Growing up, my life took a turn that I never anticipated. I found myself drawn to the streets, to the thrill of adventure and rebellion.

I was living on the edge, running with the guys from the neighborhood, trying to prove myself as someone tough to be reckoned with. I played the role well, pretending to be someone I wasn't, all while hiding behind a facade of bravado. It was all fun and games until that fateful day – the day I crossed a line that changed the trajectory of my life forever.

The crime I committed was a vehicular armed robbery. Looking back, it's hard to fathom the choices I made, the paths I walked down. But let me backtrack and share the earlier chapters of my life with you.

In my youth, I was a star in the world of sports. From 12 to 15, I dominated the field and court. Football was my realm, where my speed, agility, and catching skills made me stand out. Basketball, soccer, dodgeball – I excelled in them all. To complement my physical prowess, I even delved into the art of Tae Kwon Do, a Korean martial art known for its dynamic kicks and strikes.

Tae Kwon Do wasn't just about physical techniques; it was a philosophy that resonated with me. The discipline, the respect, the indomitable spirit – these values became part of who I was. I trained hard, donned the traditional dobok, and immersed myself in martial arts. It was a stark contrast to the path I would later take.

Fast forward to my downfall; my choices landed me behind bars. I allowed myself to be swayed by the allure of the streets, seeking validation and a sense of manhood. It wasn't about financial need; my parents provided for me. It was about proving myself to a world that seemed to demand it.

In my misguided pursuit of identity, I committed an armed robbery. Michigan's laws are harsh regarding such offenses. I was sentenced to over two decades in prison, paying the price for my choices.

But my story doesn't end here. Incarceration became a turning point, a moment of reckoning. Stripped of my freedom, I had time to reflect on the choices that led me to this point. The introspection and realization of the gravity of my actions changed me. It was a chance for redemption, an opportunity to transform the direction of my life.

Behind those prison walls, I embarked on a different kind of journey – a journey of self-discovery, growth, and redemption. It wasn't easy; facing my mistakes, confronting my past, and working toward rehabilitation required immense strength. But within the confines of those walls, I found a new purpose.

THE PRISON EXPERIENCE

Stepping into the heart of the prison after receiving my sentence for armed robbery and carjacking, I was engulfed by a wave of emotions, a blend of overwhelming trepidation and crippling anxiety. As the heavy metal doors clanged behind me, it was as though the door to my past life was slammed shut, marking the commencement of an entirely new chapter characterized by fear and the unknown.

Initially, the prison environment struck me with its stark and unwelcoming demeanor. The cold, unfeeling gray walls seemed to absorb all warmth. At the same time, the cacophony of echoing voices – both from fellow inmates and the guards – coupled with the sensation of constant scrutiny created a disorienting atmosphere that magnified the weight of my predicament. Every step I took seemed to be accompanied by a sense of confinement and suffocation, as if the walls were closing in.

The unfamiliarity of prison life was a bitter reality that I had to adapt quickly. As I navigated through the maze-like corridors, the piercing stares from other inmates intensified my anxiety. Being a newcomer, an outsider, meant I had to tread carefully, cautiously navigating the unspoken social hierarchies while grappling with the knowledge that potential dangers lurked around every corner. The uncertainty of each interaction and the ominous specter of the unknown cast a constant shadow over my thoughts.

Isolation became an omnipresent companion. The sensation of being cut off from the world I once knew, from family, friends, and familiarity, was a gnawing ache that accompanied me every day. The void left by their absence was profound, and the weight of loneliness was an unrelenting burden I carried.

The routines within the prison were a rigid dance, each day a monotonous repetition that offered minimal room for personal choice or variation. The constant lack of privacy, coupled with the unyielding watchfulness of guards and inmates, stripped away any sense of autonomy, leaving me exposed and vulnerable. The paradox of being surrounded by people while feeling profoundly alone was a duality that continually haunted me.

Simultaneously, I grappled with the heavy burden of guilt and remorse. Confronted by the undeniable reality that my choices had led me down this path, I was forced to reckon with the consequences of my actions and the pain they had inflicted on others. The guilt and shame were relentless, a constant inner turmoil that I wrestled with as I sought redemption.

Survival within the prison's confines demanded quick adaptation. I learned to keep a low profile to steer clear of unnecessary conflicts and interactions that might escalate into danger. Every word and gesture became calculated as I delicately navigated the intricate web of social dynamics, acutely aware that even a small misstep could have profound consequences.

However, amid the gloom, glimmers of hope managed to pierce through the darkness. Engaging in prison programs and educational initiatives provided a fragile sense of purpose and personal growth. While far from perfect, these opportunities offered a brief respite from the harsh reality of prison life, granting me the chance to learn, evolve, and find solace in self-improvement.

Every day was a tumultuous mix of emotions – fear, regret, loneliness, and a flicker of hope. As time progressed, I understood that surviving within these walls required physical strength and mental resilience. I held tightly onto the belief that I could change and that this experience could catalyze transformation and rehabilitation.

Despite the immense weight of my past actions and the enduring challenges that prison presented, I was resolute in facing them head-on. This journey through incarceration was just beginning, and I was determined to harness the time I had to reflect, learn, and evolve. Through introspection and self-discovery, I sought to pave a path toward redemption and the promise of a better future.

Embarking on the journey of imprisonment was an ordeal I wouldn't wish on anyone. It plunged me into an abyss of self-discovery and personal reckoning. The confines of prison walls became a metaphor for the confinements of my own choices. While I may have entered with my strengths and vulnerabilities, the system, the environment, and the constant struggle for survival tested every fiber of my being.

The early days were marked by a blend of emotions – despair, resentment, and a yearning for what once was. Once taken for granted, the concept of freedom now felt like a distant dream. The institutional atmosphere, the regimented routines, and the inherent distrust created a landscape that was foreign and dehumanizing. It was in this environment that I discovered the raw essence of resilience.

The prison hierarchy was a universe with codes and rules that evolved independently of the outside world. My entry into this world was fraught with apprehension, the unspoken tension palpable with every gaze and hushed conversation. Being a newcomer meant negotiating unspoken alliances and decoding gestures and postures while maintaining a semblance of identity and self-respect.

Isolation was a formidable adversary. The physical separation from my loved ones was mirrored by an emotional chasm that seemed impossible to bridge. The letters and occasional visits were lifelines that momentarily transported me beyond the grim reality. The echoing corridors and dimly lit cells became a testament to my yearning for connection, a constant reminder that the human spirit perseveres even in the bleakest of places.

Prison routines were a paradox – the structured monotony provided a semblance of stability while eroding individuality and autonomy. The loss of privacy was a constant reminder of my status as a captive, a stark reminder of the choices that had led me to this juncture. The ever-watchful eyes of guards and fellow inmates underscored the delicate balance between self-preservation and retaining one's sense of self.

A cloud of regret hung heavily over my thoughts. The stark realization of the pain I had inflicted upon others, the consequences of my actions – they were like shadows that followed me relentlessly. Guilt and shame were my constant companions, propelling me toward a deep exploration of my character and the pursuit of self-betterment.

Survival within prison necessitated a complex dance of adaptation and restraint. Navigating the unspoken rules, learning to gauge intentions, and exercising caution in interactions were skills honed out of necessity. While the physical challenges were palpable, the emotional turmoil often posed an equal, if not greater, threat.

Amidst the trials, moments of hope shimmered like rare gems. Engaging in programs and education provided a semblance of purpose, a reminder that growth was still possible even within concrete walls. These brief respites offered glimpses of transformation and a means of grappling with the demons within.

Every day brought mixed emotions – fear of the future, the weight of the past, and the persistent hope for change. As time continued its relentless march, I began to understand that the prison experience was a crucible, testing my resilience and my capacity for self-discovery and redemption.

The prison environment was both an oppressor and a mirror. It held a mirror of my past choices, my strengths, and my weaknesses. It demanded that I confront the darkest recesses of my character while challenging me to reclaim my sense of self-worth. The prison walls may have been unforgiving, but within their confines, I was forced to confront the duality of human nature – the potential for darkness and the enduring flame of hope.

One day, about a week into my stay in quarantine, the officers let us out to make a 15-minute phone call. I was on the fifth gallery, but I had to go down all these flights of stairs to get to the main floor and use the phone. And twenty to thirty inmates are coming from their cells and walking down the stairs. Guards are at the bottom watching the inmates, and security is at the very top to ensure that nothing happens for the most part. So, as I was walking down the stairs, this inmate behind me stepped on the back of my shoe. I know he did it intentionally because he laughed after he did it. I almost fell. The shoes are soft slippers that they give you and come off very easily. Needless to say, I knew that was the moment that I had to show that I was not the one. I turned around and immediately started whooping his behind. I whooped the hell out of him. The guards came, saw the fight, and broke it up. But fortunately, I didn't get into much trouble because they knew I was quarantined. It was my first time there and I was still learning the rules. So, the guards overlooked it. It was no big deal. They just separated us. Ever since that fight, it gave me a reputation throughout the years.

Even after five to ten years into my prison sentence, I remember people talking about that fight and how I whipped that guy so badly. The other inmates left me alone, even though I had other fights in prison. I had to show people that prison is a place where you are constantly tested. Your manhood is tested. People want to try you for whatever reason. They may not like how you look or want to get a reputation off of you because you know how to fight. They figured they'd have a reputation for not being messed with if they whooped that guy. So, it was that kind of thing constantly.

Nevertheless, prison was very unsettling, but I always knew I was better than my environment. I knew that my mother raised me better than my behavior and actions displayed. I really hated prison for so many reasons. I had no reason to be there. What I did, I knew better than to do. I was raised to know about God. My mother and grandmother were very praying people. Even as a young child, I knew better, yet I was in prison for armed robbery.

Every day I was there, I prayed and tried to find ways to better myself. I stayed in the dictionary. I would always read the dictionary, just reading, and learning words and vocabulary. I studied Spanish and also studied sign language for the hearing impaired. So now, I can speak three languages: English, sign language, and Spanish. I also became very proficient in the Bible because I read it constantly. One of my favorite verses I was raised on was what my mother always told me: do not be conformed to this world but be ye transformed by the renewing of your mind. Also, greater is He that is in you than he that is in the world, and as a man thinks, so is he.

I grew up with those scriptures. That's the kind of language my grandmother and mother always spoke to me and poured into me as a young guy, like four or five years old. They were constant. I would always hear those kinds of words. So, I guess that resonated with me when I was in prison. I knew I was better than that place. But again, prison is the worst place I've ever experienced. I was lonely. I felt isolated by the tenth power. I remember being in my cell in quarantine. I was so lonely, distraught, and desperate to find a way to change my environment. At 19 years old, it was my reality of being in prison and potentially being there for 50 years. I'm trying to wrap my brain around it all. Still, I'm hearing 25 to 50 years of being there. It was inconceivable for me to really come to grips with that mentally. I was desperate for any answers or any way of escape. I was using mind powers, or telepathy, to transcend through the walls to be at home. I was just distraught at the thought of not being able to have a life and I thought my life was over. I stood in the middle of my cell, closed my eyes, clicked my heels three times, and said, "There's no place like home, there's no place like home, there's no place like home." I said that three times. Then I opened my eyes and burst into tears when I realized I was still in prison. I would beg God and pray, "Please let me open my eyes and this just be a dream." I would go to sleep at night and just pray that prayer. And when I woke up, all this would be a dream; that I would find myself in my bed at home with my family and friends.

It took a long time for me to really come to grips with the fact that I was there and potentially could be there for the rest of my life for armed robbery. The other thing that got me and my family was that we knew I wasn't a perfect kid. I was receiving and concealing stolen property when I was 17 years old I used to do little things like take bikes and fight guys, but I never raped or murdered anybody. I never sold dope. I never shot anybody. I'm not justifying what I did because taking anybody's moped or car was stupid, and that's what I did. But I never hurt anyone. And to hear them say 25 to 50 years for armed robbery was mind-blowing. Particularly when I've seen men throughout my prison tenure come in for rape or molesting a little girl. They would get far less time than what I got. Some would only get three or five years for rape or violating a woman's or a little girl's womb. Those clowns would get five years maximum, and then they got out. They would come back as repeat offenders and beat me home. They would come back again for raping a girl and beat me home. This was the Michigan sentencing guidelines. They were very lenient on the rape crimes, which was crazy to me that they, the court system, would put more value on a car than on a little girl's or a woman's womb. So, a lot of people were very upset about that. But you have guys coming in for different kinds of crimes that you think would be more punishable by law, which was simply not the case. So, I was very upset about that, and it took a while to get over it. Even today, I struggle with all the years I lost because of this crime. I'm not minimizing what I did because what I did absolutely deserved to be punished, I deserved to serve time, no doubt about it, but 25 years to 50 was very extreme.

The prison food was horrible. Everything in it wasn't made with love. That's the first time I've ever seen brown vegetables – brown green beans, and brown peas. It looked disgusting, and it smelled like dog food. This is not an exaggeration. There's nothing good or healthy about prison food.

And on top of that, the people who were cooking or preparing the food were other inmates. They were allowed to work in the kitchen, supervised by a guard. But nevertheless, the inmates preparing the food were guys who raped people, had low values and self-esteem, or didn't love themselves. You don't know if these guys spit in your food, put something in it, dropped it on the floor, picked it up, and served it on the line. Although I'm sure they've done it before. If you didn't have someone that could send you money to go to the commissary and buy groceries or food, then you were almost subjected and forced to eat the stuff they served. Fortunately for me, my mother, father, and family ensured that I had money on my books to buy ramen noodle soups, which was the main course meal. You just "doctor it up" with other things like honey, onions, and maybe some tuna fish because they had tuna in the store. However, you're eating the same stuff every day. There's no variety of food. It's not like you're going to a supermarket. They have very little food you can eat in prison; if you don't like it, you just don't eat.

I was a person who lifted weights almost every single day. I would practice martial arts in the yard so it could stay fresh in my mind with martial arts. That's what I did. After you're in your cell for a few months, you feel like a captive. It's literally what you are. I always tell the story of how the yard doors would open at 7:30 or 7:45 to go to the yard. I remember just being so excited and anticipating the cell door opening that I was at the door, almost like a dog would be trying to get out to use the bathroom or just happy to get out of his cage to go outside and play. So the dog would be jolting at the door, jumping up and down, hollering and screaming, just trying to get out. I found myself like that after being in that cell for so long. You find yourself at the door, just waiting for them to open so you can rush out to the weighting pit, the phone, or whatever.

Quickly, I understood how animals must feel because that's what I felt like, a trapped animal in an eight-by-eight cell room. But I would lift weights daily, study my Koran, study my Bible, study the dictionary, and go to self-help groups. I went to all the self-help groups, "thinking for change", "cage your rage", "life skills", "conflict resolution", "changing criminal thinking patterns", and "mediation skills". I went to all those classes, and after being in them for so long, I mastered them so well that the warden wound up making me a lead facilitator. I was the guy who was now running the study groups for those courses and teaching other inmates. I had a very good knack for doing that. I was very effective with people and was very good at being able to describe their thought patterns and how those erroneous thoughts led them to commit crimes and eventually being imprisoned. I had a unique way of expressing and illustrating people's thoughts. I did that for most of my twenty years in prison. I was in study groups, which kept me out of trouble and from becoming institutionalized.

Because I was always doing positive things with my time, I was never one sitting around and getting into what prisoners do. For the most part, I spent my time studying, reading, and mastering the Bible, the Koran, and all the study guides, and trying to understand what I did and where I went wrong. It was therapeutic for me to teach those classes. While teaching, I learned more about myself and discovered my own errors in life. This led me to appreciate more the great family I came from. I never wanted money. I was never starving. My four older brothers were all successful. Two of them were police officers; one was an aerospace engineer with Lockheed Martin, and my other brother was a percussionist in New York who played with the Alvin Ailey Dance Theater of Harlem and played in the movie called The Cotton Club. The guy that played Herman Monster and the big guy Lurch were in the Cotton

Club, but my brother was the drummer in the movie. Also, Gregory Hines was in the Cotton Club. He was the tap-dancing guy and the main lead character in the movie.

They were friends back then, in the '80s. All my family members were successful. So, I was very confused about what had happened to me. Being in those self-help groups really helped me process my thoughts and sit down and analyze what went wrong. What I came up with and discovered was that I was entitled. I was very spoiled. I was self-centered. I felt that if I saw something and wanted it, I had a right to have it. If somebody wouldn't buy it for me, then my ignorant self-felt like I had a right to take it, that I had some kind of ownership over things that weren't mine. So, from my experiences, I'm very hard on some of the children I mentor today about being arrogant and thinking that you own the world. I'm very humble now. That experience and awakening of what went wrong caused me to do a 360 in my mind regarding humility. So, that is what I am. I'm a very humble person and love God. I always loved God. Even in my madness, I was rebellious but always loved God. I was always searching to find out who He was, who it was, or what it was. I tried to line my life up with it by tapping into my own self, thoughts, and behaviors to try to understand the higher self in me because greater is He that is in you than he that is in the world.

I would get visitors all the time. That was the other thing that kept me levelheaded and able to deal with being in prison. I would always get visits from my mother, father, and friends. It was what all inmates lived for. That's the only thing that keeps you going in prison: the commissary, the visits, and the phones. Those are the things we live for daily to survive all the years. Another of the worst parts of prison was that you were strip-searched after the visit. I remember the first time I had a visit from my mother. When the visit ended, I had to strip-search in a room. I remember the officer saying, "Hey, come on. You've got to go in this room here." It's a room in the control center where the visits are held. He opens the door.

I go into this small room that looks almost like a cell. I'm in there with a male officer, and he says to me, "Strip. Take off your clothes." So, I took my clothes off and kept on my underwear. Then he said, "Pull down your underwear. You've got to take your underwear off too." So, I take my underwear off, and he says, "Alright now. Turn around, bend over, and spread your butt cheeks apart so I can see if you're smuggling in any contraband." And I looked at him and said, "I'm not doing that." He says, "Man, come on, man. I don't have time for this. Come on. Turn around, spread, and pull your cheeks. Man, I ain't got time for this." I told him, "Man, come on. I'm not doing that. I am not. What do you think? I took something and put it up behind me." I said, I was out there with my mother, man. Come on, man. I am not doing that, bro." He tells me, "If you don't do that, I must call the sergeant to come here. You are going to wind up going to solitary confinement. They will write you a major misconduct ticket, taking time off your good time. It's going to make you spend more time in prison. In other words, they're playing with your time now, and it is not worth it, bro." So, they were really hard on me about that. Reluctantly, I submitted And when I tell you, it is one of the most humiliating things a man can ever do. That was a very hard thing to do. Unfortunately, I've done more than I can count during my twenty years in prison.

I had a great reputation in prison. People knew not to mess with me because I was a good fighter and a leader on the prison yard. I was always the guy giving advice and telling them it would be all right and they would be okay. But I was also the guy who would tear you out of the frame, so to speak, for coming to prison for raping a little girl or woman or murdering a woman, as several people I knew in Detroit did. One guy holding a crowbar made a girl jump off the Belle isle Bridge because she accidentally hit the back of his car on the bridge. I think it was on a Saturday, and it was crowded. And this clown got out of his car and scared the woman so bad that she took her baby, and they jumped into the Detroit River and drowned. She killed herself because of this clown, and he was imprisoned. The man who beat up Rosa Parks broke into her house. I think that was back in the '90s. We dealt with him because he came to prison. I was there with Dr. Jack Kevorkian. He asked me for protection because of the crowd I was running with and my power and respect in prison.

Dr. Jack was known as the assisted suicide guy. He was the one who was killing people and having people take their lives. In his mind, it was the thing to do because these people were severely damaged or incapacitated or couldn't function independently. So, he would assist them in killing themselves. When he was arrested, he hired a popular Detroit Southfield attorney named Geoffrey Fieger. While I was in prison with him. He came to me and asked me, "How much would it cost for you to give me some protection, man, because a lot of people don't like me." He was a small, older white guy, supposedly with a lot of money, with the title of doctor. He felt people would try to victimize him, rape him, or even kill him. So, he asked me to protect him, me, and my friends. We did our best, and I'll leave it at that. Those were some of the things I would do to try to help less fortunate people, but we weren't from any gangs. You would get dealt with if you were imprisoned for sexual molestation, domestic abuse and offenses against the elderly or women. That was unacceptable, even today.

Life in prison was a delicate balance of survival and self-improvement. While the backdrop was harsh and unyielding, the journey through incarceration was a quest for personal redemption. It was a journey to reconcile my actions, grapple with the past, and transform a seemingly hopeless situation into an opportunity for growth.

Imprisonment was a realm of paradoxes. It was a place of torment and introspection, isolation and connection, despair, and hope. It was a realm where the human spirit, no matter how burdened, could evolve and transcend its surroundings. The prison doors may have confined my body, but they couldn't contain the potential for change and the yearning for a better tomorrow.

CHAPTER 3
MY FATHER

I lost my father while still incarcerated. The memory of that fateful day when the officer informed me of his death remains etched in my mind. Man, when I got that news about my father, it hit me like a ton of bricks. It was like a punch in the gut, and I felt this overwhelming rush of emotions I couldn't control. I couldn't believe he was gone, and the fact that I couldn't be there to say goodbye or attend the funeral made it even harder to process.

I felt this intense sadness, like a heavy weight on my chest that wouldn't disappear. It's tough being in that place, feeling so far away from my family, and not being able to be there for them during such a difficult time. I kept replaying all those moments with my dad in my mind, wishing I had told him how much he meant to me, how much I loved him.

Grief is a weird thing, you know? It's like a roller coaster ride of emotions. One moment, I'd feel this deep sorrow; the next, I'd be angry and frustrated at the whole situation. I wanted to scream, punch something, and let it all out. But you can't do that in prison, not without consequences.

I wrote letters to my dad, even though he was gone. It was my way of talking to him, of telling him everything I wish I could have said in person. I poured my heart out on those pages, giving me some sort of release, a way to cope with the pain.

There were days when I just wanted to shut down, to block out everything and everyone. But somehow, I had to keep going and pushing through each day. It's not like you get a break from grief just because you're behind bars. It's even harder because you're stuck in this place, surrounded by walls and bars, unable to escape the pain.

I missed my dad so much, and it hurt to think that I'll never see him again, never get to hug him or hear his voice. I just had to take it one day at a time, hoping that somehow, I'll find some peace and healing while so far away from home.

My father's fame from his time with Motown and his collaborations with renowned artists like Marvin Gaye and The Dramatics had made him well-known even among the guards at the facility. It was Officer Baker who delivered the devastating news to me. I vividly recall him entering my cell and delivering the heart-wrenching message. His compassionate words and comforting embrace provided some solace, assuring me that my father's legacy as a legend would endure forever.

Despite my desire to attend my father's funeral, I had to be escorted by a guard. My brother paid a considerable sum of $500 for this privilege, the customary fee for such an arrangement. The guard assigned to take me there kindly assured me that he would remove the shackles and cuffs so that I could pay my respects to my father without such restraints. His gesture of understanding and support was deeply appreciated.

However, as the funeral approached, my hopes were dashed when another officer, Officer Johnson, informed me that he would not follow the same lenient approach. He insisted on adhering strictly to the facility's regulations, leaving me no choice but to be at the ceremony with shackles. His callousness and apparent enjoyment in delivering this news shook me, and I ultimately decided not to attend.

The local media covered the funeral live. This compounded my discomfort even more, making me hesitant to face such a solemn moment in a room filled with mourners while bound by handcuffs and shackles. The memory of that scene would have been haunting, and I wanted to preserve my last private moments with my father, free from the constraints of my incarceration.

Ultimately, the pain of not saying a final goodbye to my father at his funeral was surpassed by the desire to remember him in a more intimate and dignified setting. I chose to honor his memory in my own way, free from restraints and shielded from the prying eyes of the media. It was a painful decision I made with love and respect for my father's spirit.

This is one of my most heartfelt accounts of the complexities I faced dealing with loss while incarcerated. The conflicting emotions and difficult choices one must make in such circumstances bring forth themes of love, respect, and the desire for a dignified farewell to a departed loved one.

CHAPTER 4
FREEDOM TO WHERE?

I emerged from prison in 2012, and to my immense relief, my family stood by me, offering their unwavering support and love. But not all of my brothers shared this belief in my potential post-release success. One brother in particular expressed doubts, insinuating that I couldn't achieve without a college education or job skills. His lack of faith stung deeply, especially when I discovered he'd been speaking negatively about me behind my back.

Incarceration, however, had transformed me in profound ways. I seized the opportunity to acquire various life skills and certificates, from conflict resolution to mediation and anger management. I even became fluent in languages and nurtured entrepreneurial ideas in fitness training. Despite my newfound expertise, my brother's skepticism remained.

Yet, from 2012 to 2023, I defied his doubts, proving him wrong by amassing nearly $100,000 since my release. I carved a niche in fitness training, working with celebrities and esteemed residents of Detroit's Harbor Town Apartments, securing a weekly income of around $1,300. I supplemented this income with odd jobs like security, further bolstering my earnings.

A pivotal moment arrived when I conversed with my police officer brother. Inspired by our discussion, I established "Prison Doc, Inc.," a 501(c)3 organization. Drawing from my prison experiences and critical thinking certifications, I aimed to mentor children and families, unafraid to visit their homes and offer guidance. I adopted the moniker "prison doctor" to symbolize my role in transforming lives through love, affirmations, and positive reinforcement.

Over the years, I engaged in over two thousand house calls, potentially diverting young people aged six to eighteen from a path toward prison or worse. My organization boasted an impressive

90% success rate, garnering recognition from influential figures such as Ambassador Andrew Young and even the White House.

Social media platforms, TikTok in particular, emerged as powerful tools to raise awareness about my efforts, accumulating over one-hundred million views. While funding remained useful, it never dictated our mission, which was to save children's lives regardless of politics, race, or wealth.

Lamentably, I observed a decline in parental involvement due to the allure of social media and the corrosive influence of contemporary music, replete with derogatory language, especially towards women. This shift from the values fought for by our forefathers deeply troubled me.

A particular incident stands out from my initial week of freedom: observing two men smoking weed next to me at a traffic light, an infant seated in the back. Social media platforms abounded with explicit content, including suggestive dances and provocative images posted by women. My concerns deepened as I witnessed the erosion of values and respect that previous generations had fought to uphold.

In the face of these challenges, my organization's core mission endured: to positively impact children's lives, illuminating their path towards hope and success. The blessings in my life fostered both pride and humility. My unwavering commitment to aiding others and instigating meaningful change in the world remained steadfast.

As for my chosen title, "The Prison Dr.," allow me to elaborate. In a similar vein to how specialized doctors emerge from intensive medical training, my two decades within "Prison School" have equipped me with unparalleled expertise. Armed with three master's degrees, I've delved into Prisonology and the identification of criminal thinking patterns. My collection of certificates spans diverse domains, from life skills to anger management, mediation, and criminal thought processes. Throughout my incarceration, I immersed myself in self-help courses, eventually taking on the role of a lead facilitator, guiding fellow inmates. My interactions spanned the gamut of criminals, from murderers to politicians.

Upon my reintegration into society, I faced the challenges posed by my criminal record and limited formal education. While my name might not be adorned with the conventional titles like Ph.D., M.B.A., MD, or B.S., I possess a G.E.D. that symbolizes my resolve. Rather than capitulating to these constraints, I harnessed the skills I'd cultivated during my time behind bars. My engagement in martial arts, weightlifting, and teaching fortified my transformation. Years of involvement in martial arts and leadership within study groups, coupled with my certification as a fitness instructor, positioned me to make a tangible difference. By incorporating self-defense training, I aimed to counteract the disturbing surge in violence and misguided behaviors among our youth.

Navigating the uncharted territory beyond the prison's walls demanded time; the world had evolved in ways that diverged significantly from my recollections. Witnessing the prevalence of men wearing sagging pants, once indicative of specific individuals, had become disconcertingly commonplace. The sexualization of women's attire and the rampant use of derogatory language further underscored the shift in societal norms. The surge in explicit music, coupled with drug use and the proliferation of disrespectful attitudes towards women, painted a stark picture of the degradation of values and standards that generations before us had fought to uphold.

In the face of these challenges, the crux of my organization's mission persevered: to instill positive impacts on the lives of children, guiding them towards the beacon of hope and achievement. The blessings that graced my life elicited both pride and humility. My unwavering commitment to aiding others and instigating meaningful change in the world remained steadfast.

CHAPTER 5
MY SPIRITUAL WALK

And so, my spirit's journey commenced, which I suppose was instigated by my upbringing in a family devoted to prayer. It all traces back to my mother and grandmother, who was born into a Christian tradition and nurtured in its ways. As a young boy, our routine involved attending church together. My brothers and I, mere toddlers then, were already introduced to the Baptist church scene in Detroit, Michigan. This became a weekly ritual, and to this very day, our family maintains its dedication to prayer as an integral aspect of our lives. I hold a profound conviction in the potency of prayer and its tangible effects.

From my grandmother's lips and my mother's heart, I absorbed the wisdom of phrases like " greater is He that is in you than he that is in the world." This language was woven into my upbringing, an omnipresent reminder of our spiritual strength. Other verses, such as "You shall be the head and not the tail" and "Do not be unequally yoked," reverberated in my ears and resided in my heart throughout my formative years.

These lessons stuck with me as I matured into adulthood, even during personal turmoil and confusion. Even amid my struggles, those words remained etched in my consciousness. I've always believed that my mother and grandmother's seeds of spirituality were bound to sprout one day. They imparted the notion that within us lies an untapped reservoir of potential and strength, a dormant greatness waiting to be unleashed. This inner power and spirit could empower us to surmount even the most daunting challenges if harnessed.

This upbringing was foundational, and its influence on me was unwavering. Consequently, when I found myself incarcerated, those seeds of faith still dwelled within me, resilient in the face of my inner turmoil. Amidst the hardships, the core of my belief was that the word of God resided within me and that His presence was always with me. Even though I did wrong things, I was consciously aware that I had a self-sabotaging, low self-esteem attitude towards life. And so I did things that I knew were wrong. I was not oblivious to what I did and was fully aware that the things I did were unacceptable to God. It was not a righteous thing to do. But because of my weakness, I fell victim to sin, as I still do every day; it's gotten stronger in the types of mistakes I make. I don't do the same things I did as a child. Obviously, the same mistakes I don't make anymore, but I still do make mistakes. So, I carried that spirit, knowing that there was something in me, a greater purpose, a higher calling in my life. I carried that, that knowledge and that spirit, you know, even when I was in prison, and it helped me to be able to overcome 20 years of incarceration. People always ask me Man, how did you do it? How did you survive 20 years in prison? My answer is the same every single time. It wasn't me. It was God. I don't know how I did it, but I can tell you that it wasn't me.

So, you know, if it hadn't been for God and the faith that my grandmother and mother had instilled in me during my youth, I wouldn't have navigated those 20 years with the success I managed to achieve. So, when I entered prison, there was a shift in my circumstances; I became a member of the Nation of Islam. This occurred back in 1992 or 1993 if I recall correctly. I joined the Nation of Islam while I was incarcerated.

The turning point came when I was spotted in the prison yard practicing martial arts, going through my forms, and perfecting my techniques. One day, while engrossed in my martial arts practice, members of the Nation of Islam noticed me. They approached me and expressed interest, saying, "Hey, man, could you teach us how to do that?" I readily agreed and said, "Yeah, sure."

As a newcomer to the prison environment, I navigated an unfamiliar landscape. Everything was new and overwhelming, from the routines to the social dynamics. Amidst the challenges and uncertainties, an unexpected opportunity arose that would profoundly shape my journey in prison.

Approached by members of the Fruit of Islam within the Nation of Islam, I was invited to share my expertise in martial arts and self-defense. It was a modest start, a simple way to contribute to the prison community. I eagerly accepted because I was willing to connect and make a positive impact. Little did I know that this initial decision would lead me down a path of personal transformation and spiritual exploration.

Over the months, as I taught martial arts techniques and self-defense skills, I began to establish connections with these individuals who were part of the Nation of Islam. As we spent time together in training sessions, I became increasingly intrigued by their beliefs, values, and way of life. Their energy and unity were palpable, and I was drawn into their world.

The conversations we shared extended beyond physical training. They spoke passionately about their faith, their community, and their commitment to bettering themselves and the lives of those around them. Their knowledge of black History, culture, and the struggles that defined our collective past was impressive. Evidently, they held a deep respect for their roots. They were dedicated to promoting positivity and unity within the prison environment.

What resonated most with me were their values. They advocated for the dignity and respect of women, fostering a culture of modesty and mutual respect. This resonated deeply with the values my family and upbringing instilled in me. The Nation of Islam members condemned behaviors perpetuating harm and division, such as infidelity, promiscuity, and absentee parenting. Their stand against violence and abuse, especially towards women, aligned with my principles and experiences.

Delving further into their teachings, I learned about prominent figures from African American History who had left an indelible mark on society. Icons like Martin Luther King Jr., Louis

Farrakhan, W.E.B. Du Bois, and Rosa Parks were celebrated for their courage, advocacy, and contributions. Through the Nation of Islam, I understood the rich tapestry of achievements woven by black individuals throughout History.

In retrospect, my initial decision to teach martial arts opened the door to a journey of self-discovery and spiritual exploration within the prison walls. The connections I forged, the values I embraced, and the knowledge I gained from the Nation of Islam played an instrumental role in shaping the person I would become during my time incarcerated.

Within a short period, I became a member of the Nation of Islam. This decision was largely influenced by the stark reality of prison life. Behind bars, positivity and spirituality were rare commodities. The environment was devoid of righteousness, filled instead with individuals who had committed various crimes and transgressions. It was a space populated by convicts and felons, each bearing the weight of their regrettable actions.

Amidst this darkness, discovering a community that spoke about righteousness, God, and spiritual upliftment was like finding an oasis in a desert. The teachings of the Nation of Islam resonated deeply with me. Their messages of hope, empowerment, and the belief that the divine within us is stronger than the world's negativity reverberated through my being. In a place where negativity thrived, these messages shone as beacons of light.

Embracing the Nation of Islam meant embracing a brotherhood that starkly contrasts the unrighteousness that pervaded the prison environment. It was a sanctuary where discussions centered around righteousness, God's presence, and the strength within us to overcome challenges. These conversations were a breath of fresh air, a reprieve from the bleakness that had become the norm.

My involvement with the Nation of Islam became a transformative journey. The organization not only provided a spiritual foundation but also instilled in me a deeper understanding of African American History and culture. Their teachings shed light on the struggles of our people, both in the past and present. Through their guidance, I gained discipline, became more conscientious, and learned to navigate life's complexities with renewed purpose.

The Nation of Islam was more than a religious movement; it was a beacon of empowerment for individuals seeking a positive path amidst adversity.

My time with the Nation of Islam was pivotal in my prison experience. It offered me solace, a sense of belonging, and the tools to grow as an individual. The organization's teachings enriched my understanding of History, culture, and the enduring spirit of resilience that has defined the African American community. Through its teachings, I found strength, purpose, and the resolve to better myself, even within the confines of incarceration.

Moreover, the Nation of Islam strongly emphasizes self-improvement and discipline. Their followers are encouraged to pursue education, knowledge, and skills to uplift themselves and their communities. By abstaining from vices such as alcohol, drugs, and promiscuous behavior, adherents strive for clean and disciplined living. Pursuing personal growth aims to cultivate capable leaders and active societal contributors.

The teachings of the Nation of Islam have had a profound impact on its followers, fostering a strong sense of black identity and empowerment. Their distinctive blend of black nationalism and Islamic principles has sparked widespread attention and debate, reflecting the complex History of racial relations in the United States. As the movement continues to evolve, its teachings remain a vital aspect of its identity, influencing the beliefs and actions of its adherents and shaping discussions on race, identity, and religion in American society.

To avoid sweeping generalizations about any racial or ethnic group's behaviors or beliefs. I found out that many black inmates were drawn to the Nation of Islam. One of the reasons was the identity and sense of belonging they offered. The Nation of Islam provided a strong community and a sense of pride in the black heritage. The organization's emphasis on camaraderie and solidarity appealed to the prison environment where black inmates felt disconnected or marginalized.

Social support was another reason for gravitating toward the Nation of Islam. Prison life is a harsh and isolating environment; the Nation of Islam offered support networks and a feeling of brotherhood, which comforted black inmates seeking companionship and understanding. The more I understood the Nation of Islam, the more I realized their focus was on addressing social and racial injustices and a Spiritual path to serving

God. Most of us have experienced discrimination or systemic inequalities in our lives. Some of us were serving longer sentences that should have been shortened or did not merit the type of offense committed. The Nation of Islam's emphasis on advocating for social justice resonated with most of us and was relevant to our experiences. Another aspect was our spiritual growth. Many people, including me, learned a lot about God and in a different light. The Nation of Islam encouraged self-improvement, discipline, and education, providing hope for a better future and a path toward rehabilitation for those seeking personal development and transformation. We also needed safety and protection. In the prison environment, where security can be a concern, a sense of security and protection was enticing to those who needed it, but for me, having a martial arts background did not need it. I was relied upon by my brothers to provide it instead.

Nevertheless, my affiliation today lies outside the Nation of Islam. I've embraced Christianity, fully believing in the power and majesty of Jesus Christ. In every action I take, I acknowledge Him. The Nation of Islam also acknowledges Jesus, but their perspective on Him differs somewhat from the Christian community's view. While the variations aren't monumental, they're there, and I noticed those nuances, prompting my return to Christianity. However, it's important to note that my shift doesn't mean I hold any negative sentiments toward the Nation of Islam. They're an admirable organization composed of good-hearted individuals who excel in their endeavors.

As for the Bible, it holds a significant place in my heart. I'm an avid reader of the Bible, but I approach it cautiously. It's no secret that the Bible has undergone numerous revisions over time, and alterations have been made to its contents. My respect for the Bible remains steadfast, and as a Christian, I wholeheartedly acknowledge Jesus Christ as Lord. However, I recognize the historical evolution of the Bible and am mindful of its changing nature.

Similarly, my stance on the Quran is akin to my perspective on the Bible. While I believe the Quran holds truths, I acknowledge that it has also experienced modifications and revisions. This isn't intended to spark a debate on what's right or wrong or what you believe versus what I believe as individuals deeply connected to our faiths.

It's essential to emphasize my independent thinking and individuality. I'm not one to be swayed by others' opinions or told what to think or believe. My convictions are mine, and I firmly believe God transcends any religious boundary. God isn't confined to a church, a mosque, or a temple – He's omnipresent. I've broken down the walls of any religious dogma or organization, understanding that God's essence can't be contained. I believe God is simply God, beyond the labels and affiliations.

I stand proudly as who I am, embracing my beliefs. I don't feel the need to pigeonhole myself into a religious group. While I identify as a Christian when asked about my religion, I'm acutely aware that God isn't defined by any particular faith. God isn't a Christian, a Muslim, or a Buddhist; God is God. The trappings of religion and its associated politics don't captivate me. The debate about who's right or wrong and which religion is superior doesn't hold much weight in my worldview. What truly matters to me is the conduct of individuals – treating each other with kindness, love, and respect.

My life is marked by prayer, a constant connection with the divine. I dedicate time to prayer, meditation, and seeking wisdom, knowledge, and understanding from God. However, I don't claim to be a religious or spiritual leader. I'm just a regular guy who places faith in God and believes in the goodness of people. I genuinely love humanity, hoping to witness acts of righteousness and happiness. I yearn for people to find success and treat one another well. This is the essence of my purpose – spreading love, unity, and understanding. In a world marred by division, hatred, and bitterness, I strive to foster connection, unity, and love among people.

I don't get tangled up in all that stuff, my friend. I'm just a guy who grew up on the streets and went through rough patches in my youth that I regret today. But you know what? Those experiences they've molded me into a better, stronger individual. It's not like I negatively regret them if you catch my drift. They were part of my journey and destiny and helped shape the person I've become – someone more resilient and aware.

I'm not harboring bitterness or anger, though. I genuinely care about people. I want to see folks doing right by each other, treating each other with kindness and respect. It's my thing, you know? And prayer, man, that's something I truly believe in. The spirit of God, it resides in all of us. And I genuinely think that if we let that spirit guide us, lead us, society would be in a much better place.

That's why I focus on loving people, being there for them, setting an example. I want to be a positive influence, a role model and show that none of us is perfect. I'm certainly not. I stumble and make my fair share of mistakes even today. But the key is to learn from them and not keep making the same ones repeatedly.

That's my deal; I strive to be better, lend a hand to others when possible, and be decent. That's what I'm all about – no aspirations of being a preacher, pastor, or anything like that. I'm just me, just an individual trying to be good and spread a bit of positivity. That's all I aim to do. Living by those principles that's my game plan. I'm just a regular guy, an individual. No fancy titles or anything. Just me, being good and hoping to make a positive impact in any way possible.

CHAPTER 6
SOLUTIONS

Although, I work with all children, my role centers on assisting primarily African American youth, a task I view as significant. We all must acknowledge the diverse challenges and strengths that different races encounter. My primary objective is to guide these young African Americans away from harmful paths, such as involvement in street life and negative behaviors. Additionally, I strive to ignite their passion for education and encourage them to set an example for the future.

The process begins with personal visits to the homes of black families. This approach allows me to establish connections with these young individuals in a relaxed environment where they feel at ease. However, these visits have unveiled a concerning pattern. An overwhelming 80% of the families I visit are headed by single mothers with no male presence. These resilient single black women are courageously raising young black boys by themselves. It's a formidable task, irrespective of their ethnicity. The real challenge is that these boys lack positive male role models, a crucial factor in their development.

Thus, my work revolves around positively influencing their lives and striving to bridge this gap. I endeavor to understand these families' unique challenges and collaborate with them to support the next generation. By addressing these challenges and providing mentorship, I aim to contribute to the growth and well-being of these young African Americans and, ultimately, the betterment of the community as a whole.

In the realm of young black men's involvement in street gangs, we're confronted with a complex web of interconnected factors contributing to this troubling phenomenon. Among these factors, one stands out as a significant driver: the absence of positive role models and supportive systems in their lives. These young men often come of age in poor neighborhoods, where access to quality education, viable job opportunities, and essential social services is limited. As a result, they frequently experience a sense of isolation and detachment from the broader societal fabric.

In this context, the allure of street gangs can be attributed to a profound need for belonging and identity. These gangs offer a sense of purpose and camaraderie that might be missing due to fractured family structures, absent fathers, or other personal challenges at home. Moreover, the appeal of financial gain and authority cannot be underestimated. Many of these young men grapple with economic hardships. They might perceive gang affiliation as a potential escape from poverty or a way to provide for their families. The allure of quick monetary rewards through illicit activities, such as drug trade, becomes even more enticing when legitimate employment prospects are scarce.

Understanding this backdrop of challenges and motivations, we can see how the multifaceted dynamics of poverty, familial instability, and limited opportunities contribute to the complex decision-making process that draws young black men into street gangs. Addressing this issue requires comprehensive efforts that encompass law enforcement, community support, education, economic empowerment, and mentorship to provide these young individuals with viable alternatives and pathways toward a brighter future.

Furthermore, the glamorization of gang culture across media, music, and movies significantly contributes to the attraction exerted by gangs on young individuals. These portrayals often romanticize violence and criminal behavior, rendering them appealing to marginalized youth in search of recognition and respect. Peer pressure and a need for protection also wield substantial influence. Gang membership might be perceived as a survival mechanism in neighborhoods rife with violence, offering safeguards against rival factions. Peer pressure compels young men into impulsive decisions, believing that joining a gang will elevate their social status and shield them from harm.

Moreover, disadvantaged communities lacking positive alternatives and recreational outlets leave young black men scant opportunities for personal growth and development. Street gangs become an escape from monotony, lacking constructive avenues and encouraging role models, providing a semblance of purpose and camaraderie. Tackling the issue of young black men succumbing to gang involvement necessitates a multifaceted approach. This entails improved educational prospects, vocational training, and community programs that advocate for positive alternatives, fostering a sense of belonging beyond gang culture. Additionally, concerted efforts must be made to counteract the glorification of gangs in media and challenge stereotypes perpetuating the notion that criminal conduct leads to success and esteem. Creating safer neighborhoods and addressing root causes of poverty and inequality are pivotal steps in deterring gang affiliation, enabling young black men to make constructive life choices.

Being a black man, I'm acutely aware of how the media holds significant sway over the prevalence of gang culture within our community. This influence demands our attention due to its complex impact on young individuals. It's evident to me how various forms of media—whether on television, in movies, or through music—tend to glamorize and idealize the world of gangs. These portrayals often depict gang members as powerful and respected figures leading thrilling lives. This portrayal's allure is particularly strong for those who might feel marginalized or overlooked, as it beckons us toward an illusory sense of belonging and recognition.

Media frequently depicts tight-knit gang communities and loyalty, painting a picture appealing to individuals searching for a sense of identity and purpose. Especially for those who feel disconnected from mainstream society or are dealing with challenges within their families, the projected idea of brotherhood or sisterhood assumes a role of immense significance. It becomes a lifeline for those struggling to find their place.

Understanding how media shapes perceptions and aspirations within our community, it's clear that addressing the glamorization of gang life in media representation becomes a critical aspect of steering young individuals away from these destructive paths. By offering more diverse and accurate portrayals of success and empowerment, we can counter the allure of gang culture and provide a more hopeful and realistic vision for our youth.

It is important not to overlook the media's role in perpetuating specific social norms and peer pressure surrounding gang culture. The prevalence and acceptance portrayed in media can be deeply disheartening. The pressure to conform and attain respect can be overwhelming. Moreover, portraying violence as a means of conflict resolution or empowerment is deeply unsettling. For disempowered people, this portrayal can cultivate the mistaken belief that resorting to violence represents the sole path to control or respect. Certain lyrics glamorize criminal conduct and endorse aggression even within music, particularly in hip-hop and rap. Witnessing the influence of these messages on the choices made by some young individuals is disconcerting. The impact has been amplified by social media, with gang members leveraging platforms to showcase their lifestyle, recruit new members, and normalize violence—an alarming trend that demands attention.

As a black man, I know the media isn't the sole factor influencing these decisions. We confront socioeconomic factors, family dynamics, and peer pressure. However, we mustn't disregard the media's role in shaping our youth's minds. To address this, a collective effort is necessary. As black men, we must strive for responsible portrayals of our community. We should offer positive alternatives, showcase success stories, and provide education and growth opportunities. Countering the glamorization of gang culture with the truth about its consequences is crucial.

Encouraging our young ones to find their identity and purpose through positive means, distancing them from the perils of gang life, is vital. We can guide our youth away from destructive paths by supporting one another, being strong role models, and fostering community collaboration. We can aid them in understanding that genuine strength emerges from unity, education, and personal development. Let's stand with them, guide them, and become the change we wish to witness in our community.

The older generation excelled in this regard. In the past, there was always an adult male figure in households. A man would answer if one were to traverse the block and knock on doors. Nowadays, men are conspicuously absent from around 80% of households on an average block in the neighborhood. The figure of the father opening the door has waned. There was a time when women refrained from answering the door for safety reasons; the men did so. Regrettably, present-day black men face daily emasculation. The once commanding Black man with a resonant voice, who represented a family to be reckoned with, is now an extinct figure. Weakness has replaced strength as men shirk their responsibility and retreat from leadership. Society views men as burdens rather than valuable contributors. Being a father or husband no longer holds appeal. A man who openly embraces family life is met with perplexed looks as if he's a relic of the past.

This is the narrative being projected. Even black women do not fare much better. Modern times have seen women embracing a sense of liberation. Present notions of allure often revolve around showing more skin than substance. This shift, stemming from generations of judgment and objectification by men, is a reaction to a long history of adversity. However, excessive exposure to their bodies can lead to further objectification, diminishing appreciation for their character and intelligence. Attracting a man is not solely about looks; our intellect, character, and thoughts hold more weight. Unfortunately, in our black community, the provocative way some women dress often overshadows their true selves. Our observant children internalize this and adapt to it. They perceive the absence of fathers and the priorities reflected in women's attire and become reflections of these circumstances. They absorb these messages, understanding that their fathers are absent and their mothers struggle to provide, sometimes seeking companionship.

I am not advocating for segregation. I firmly believe in coexistence, respecting each other's preferences while celebrating our diversity. Unity among black people is a beautiful thing. Demonstrating our beauty to other communities necessitates first embracing our need for unity. While the desire to prove ourselves to others is valid, it sometimes leads us to overemphasize appearances, spending unwisely on outward appearances. Accepting our blackness as comfortable remains a challenge. Darker skin is often linked with feelings of ugliness, while lighter skin is considered more attractive. There's an inclination to straighten our hair to conform to Eurocentric standards. This internalized bias is problematic. Our natural features, hair, skin, noses, and lips reflect divine creation. We must embrace ourselves as we were made.

This doesn't mean rejecting self-care or enhancing our appearance. However, we must strike a balance. Unfortunately, contemporary black culture sometimes veers into excess. We risk losing sight of what a genuine black woman looks like. This false narrative pervades, and the further we stray from authenticity, the more our children internalize this distortion. If this trend continues, we risk losing the essence of the authentic black woman.

Our black men have indeed faltered. Our communities have witnessed a retreat from civic responsibility. Concern for others has dwindled. Communal citizenship among black men is sparse. Acts of service and care for neighbors have given way to a mind-your-own-business attitude. We've become a people who turn away from domestic violence and crimes happening before us. This detachment starkly contrasts the generations before us, who actively intervened. Today, we remain indifferent, claiming it's not our concern. This needs to change.

As black men, we must rise above fear and embrace a genuine sense of self-love. This journey begins with a deep understanding of our history, our ancestors' struggles, and the roots that have shaped us. It's crucial not to allow anyone to belittle the significance of our past. By immersing ourselves in our heritage, connecting with our spirituality and faith, and acknowledging our connections to our cultural identity and beliefs, we fortify our sense of self.

As we navigate life, embracing fatherhood becomes integral to our growth. Embodying the role of a family man and upholding commitment and marriage calls for maturity and evolution. Letting go of distractions like video games and resisting trends like sagging pants become steps toward prioritizing our families and responsibilities.

An equally important part of this journey is our approach to music. Rejecting music that disrespects and degrades women is a way of demonstrating respect and advocating for equality. Instead of allowing jealousy and hatred to divide us, let's rise above and foster a culture of unity. Rather than tearing each other down, we should actively work to uplift and support one another.

Understanding these principles within the larger context of our lives as black men allows us to craft a path of growth, self-empowerment, and positive influence. By embracing our history, valuing our roles within our families and communities, and embodying respect and unity, we contribute to a stronger and more empowered collective future.

During our journey as black men, a troubling issue persists—self-hatred, which seems to affect us more profoundly than any other racial group. It's high time we draw lessons from other communities prioritizing mutual support and empowerment. We must staunchly reject the damaging trend of not standing by our people. The concept of unity needs a revival involving actively supporting black businesses and championing education within our community. It's imperative that we put an end to the erosion of our cultural identity on social media platforms.

We need to reconsider our perceptions of attractiveness and what it truly means. The provocative dressing trend may not genuinely reflect our beauty; rather, it can detract from our character. The time has come for us to evolve, placing substance over superficiality and directing our attention toward the core values of family and community.

Our black identity is too precious to be defined by outsiders. True authenticity emanates from within. To nurture this authenticity, we must delve into self-study, exploring our history, ancestral roots, and the principles underpinning our heritage. This knowledge will serve as the foundation for building the genuine and authentic black man you aspire to become. Through this journey, we reclaim our strength, pride, and sense of belonging, shaping a legacy that honors our past and propels us into a brighter future.

END NOTES

Printed in Great Britain
by Amazon